The Asparagus Feast

The Hugh MacLennan Poetry Series

Editors: Nathalie Cooke and Joan Harcourt
Selection Committee: Donald H. Akenson,
Philip Cercone, Eric Ormsby, Carolyn Smart,
and Tracy Ware

THE

ASPARAGUS

FEAST

S.P. Zitner

McGill-Queen's University Press
Montreal & Kingston · London · Ithaca

© McGill-Queen's University Press 1999
ISBN 0-7735-1903-3

Legal deposit fourth quarter 1999
Bibliothèque nationale du Québec

Printed in Canada on acid-free paper

McGill-Queen's University Press acknowledges the financial support of the
Government of Canada through the Book Publishing
Industry Development Program (BPIDP) for its activities.
We also acknowledge the support of the Canada Council
for the Arts for our publishing program.

Canadä

Canadian Cataloguing in Publication Data

Zitner, Sheldon P.
The asparagus feast
Poems.
ISBN 0-7735-1903-3
I. Title
PS8599.I67A86 1999   C811'.54   C99-900830-7
PR9199.3.Z48A76 1999

This book was typeset
by Typo Litho Composition Inc.
in 10.5/13 Minion.

for Julia

CONTENTS

ONE

THE NEIGHBOURHOOD IN PHASES

i: mercurial

No spring here, but a repertoire of climates.
The crocus tunnels into exile;
days from each season pelt, thaw, burn and tweak
designer weathervanes and noses
until May – permissive and conditional.

ii: lyric

Charles Street, July.
A butter-yellow shimmers down
through the leafy openwork of Freeman maples
in which some phrases we forgot
have settled, singing.

iii: bizarre

Rags of autumnal mist, the haze of traffic,
the stale of vent and grating,
the bronchial wheeze of sleepers,
restless, bedded down in headlines:
sour exhalations of affluence.

iv: martial

Gauleiter of winter, black-booted Cold
goose-steps along Bloor Street. His neon ribbons
glitter back from fashionable vitrines.
But the street is empty.
Conquered too often, the citizen evades commands.

for Charlotte

Compared to fashionable elsewheres,
it is only someplace – dully so –
in the apologetic manner of the region:
florid textiles allaying the folktale winters,
dark panelling its brief history.
Soon it will be attic stuff or worse,
having become as odd as its social moment;
think of arras and prie-dieu. But here and now,
the ephemeral assembles in a chord:
yellow carpets coddle the tepid noons
where guests who will doze on by lamplight
linger in the shapes of chairs.
Whatever should be said
looks down from frames and bindings.
Here and Now, it is just that – and one's own –
a place where Elsewhere, Was, and Will Be,
are benignly mum.

Below the martial nattiness of knives
braced in ranks against a magnetic bar
(the dapper sliver of the boning knife,
the *gravitas* of the chopping knife),
this homely factotum lies heavily on its side,
a wide peasant face grayed with work,
save for the silver slick of the working edge,
ground for severing without tearing –
clean, bloodless, almost unfelt.
Hefting the cleaver, I ponder the device:
function, but without purpose, guile or anger.
My hand's the danger.

THE BLUE VASE

for Julia

A quarter-century in boxes. I mope about,
the long-time and still briefly Occupant,
envying the squat attendance of household things
and the indifference of beloved objects.
I think of the blue Song vase, and see it –
substance as stillness – hovering,
lustrous and immaterial as a hologram:
robin's-egg blue of boyhood;
della Robbia blue of hilltown afternoons;
and, after sleeplessness, dawn's milky blue,
like your veins as a newborn;
the storm-blue of night's self-judgment;
and in my illness, when the pale nurse came
(the one with the eyes, you called her),
the blue that summons distances –
blue illusion of time possessed.

Walking along the street we used to take
to the cafe where you loved the little sandwiches
and the lingonberry jam, I heard behind me
two pairs of footsteps – one pair lighter, faster –
and then a child's voice, daughterly,
so familiar that it seemed hallucination.
I didn't turn.
It wasn't us going on Sunday to the Danes'.

ON HEARING THE *INTERNATIONALE* AT
THE BLOOR STREET SUBWAY STATION

At first I didn't recognize it,
then was surprised I did –
that iron anthem of Soviet May Days,
marching song and dirge of the oppressed,
cradle song of the future,
once whistled for courage in Spandau by the tortured,
and by the torturers in the Lubianka,
now a buskers' turn for querulous flute and violin,
but with the passion of all four Internationals
drained out of it – the heroic in falsetto.
Still a catchy tune, sardonically revamped,
late Shostakovich.

From across the rows of tracks and pillars,
the buskers (more skilled as the economy worsens),
are indistinct. Whose dumb idea was this –
emigrés being ironic or nostalgic,
clever sophomores out to twit the public?
The public is not mocked. No one pays attention
let alone the small change that they'd give
to bagpipes wheedling *Amazing Grace*
or an alto sax high on *Sweet Lorraine*.
With so many refugees here from the former Utopias,
you'd have thought that someone would protest.
Nothing. Even the cops, who twenty years ago
would have been on the case like a shot,
stroll by, unknowing, vaguely in step with it.

Just so did Homer put paid to the "Matter of Troy" –
with far-seeing Teiresias warning ruthless Ulysses
to shoulder one of the oars that had brought him home
in spite of heroes, gods, and demons,
and carry it inland till no one knew its use.

Profane violations of the taboo against naming,
attributions of unlikely habits to public officials,
and the rest of us told where to shove
an impersonal pronoun, antecedent understood.
This from a Nutso trudging east on Bloor Street,
stopping to gesticulate at corners
as if to the public, but most private.
Not for Nutso the wonders of the Creation
(himself one), nor the equal wonders of the Fall
in this incorrigible city: the smog-capped towers,
the hustle of cabs exploding puddles,
rushing deal-makers to their deals,
the sorrowing stares in Nutso's direction
by the old girl who peddles red-hots,
the triumph on jackal faces
above headlines hawked by averted eyes.
Not for Nutso. This morning not for me.

Latte and Beige,
our resident queens
but only on week-ends –
from Monday to Friday
unremarkable neighbors
in the graycollar midrise
I recently left:
how festive they were,
with their doo-wah-doo lingo
and street *politesse,*
wide lovelorn mouths
pouting down at their sequins,
slit-skirts and spike heels.
I admired their facing
beatings with only
the spinster's defense
of handbag-and-screech –
holding true to illusion –
though their working-day fists
might have fought off the laddies
who came in from Cabbagetown
righteous on beer.
And I had to admire
how they blended their bruises
into blush and mascara
and got on with the night.

How poised their farewells
and their mocking distaste,
when I told them I'd moved
and had outrun the roaches!

A white porcelain bowl is glowing,
brimming with freshly sliced tomatoes,
salmon-pink, mouth-pink, pink as rouge,
a tender pile-up of toy wagon wheels
draped over one another; delicious-looking
save for the hard white hub of one
which the solemn counterwoman at the diner,
who knows a yid when she sees one,
fastidiously extracts for my ham and cheese;
chewing which, I consider the seeds of the tomato,
slippery, hard, prolific, intractable.

Hats for pinheads, goldilocks and cretins:
a glum fedora, a top hat déclassé,
avuncular caps, a cloche that never told
the hour of love, and two morose berets.

Maybe Larry or Pegeen would like them.

For the cheerfully practical nether end, shoes:
brogue, tennis, pumps, bunion-cheeked couples
in hale old age, shining young misfits,
matronly hoofs with tongues and a falsetto.

They might fit Brian or Maxine.

And everything for what goes in between,
hanging on pipe-racks, a populous emptiness
of lives remembered in small wrinkles,
as though the whole congregation Homo Faber
had just sung out, "Don't touch me, January";
or, "Like me, love me, Other," and leaped together
joyfully dream-naked through the ceiling.

Harry with Nadine.

You have to check out this oracular junk.
It is humanized by wear and care
and monthly reductions until it's charity:
mistakes once dear that still tempt someone else
to make them and to pay for.

Jason or Kathleen perhaps.

CAFETERIA

for Joan Lubin Smucker

Hers unmistakably, the brave jet hair
severely cut, a dark Achaean helmet,
hers the rose complexion, pecan and rose,
face aquiline, expressive as the sky –

an apparition glimpsed across noisy tables.
She holds her head as when she argued causes,
or, drugged for death, she cursed its coming:
dear quicksilver talker, at once and still cherished.

Rising, she vanishes in someone else's profile,
in the coarse bravura of someone else's mouth.
Flesh offers only illusions of the nonpareil.
Anywhere leads away. We shall not meet.

Not clear to my soul. The ways to it clogged
by a debris of cage – chairs, walls that dogged
the shadows I hunted day in. Or worse, the ways
   overgrown
by these objects, which are as much flesh as my own;
I sit, a chair-like object in a chair,
read by a light-bulb whose paralytic stare
undoes the small pretensions of the place.
Gestures of a room: the servant face
of tables, cigarettes that would burn again and whistle
something under ashes, the sallow lamplight.
They hesitate a sentiment but fail
against the dark and the arrested hail
of lights that ward the city.
                      Mazda! Mazda!
In the north, where it is mountainous, a river
smoulders continuously over winged drums,
whirling toward accidents of wire and partial vacuums.
Something, it is not water, diminishes,
comes burning to this far-off emptiness.

From shoal to shoal of concrete balconies,
light seeps into the courtyard;
the neap tide of city morning
fills the bay of brick and glass.
A reading lamp in its yellow shawl,
the chromium ram's head of a motor-bike
tethered ten storeys up,
record the eccentricity of human presence.
In the damp distance, a towered crane,
colossal mistranslation of the arm,
searches the air.

All night he has dozed and waked,
stumbling uphill through sleep.
Like headlights in the courtyard,
forgiveness flares, goes black.
All night he has dozed and waked.
Not so his daughter, making her first visit,
curled on her camping-cot
inside the blue chrysalis of her bedroll,
worn asleep early by the barrenness
of naked floors and unlidded windows,
tokens of other losses.

Waking to her snickery breathing
(head cold?) he hears no wakefulness,
no calling out of nightmare
to him or to the emptiness beside him.
Then, as if at fortune in a dream,
she smiles, turns, settling again.
A pebble of her ninth-year's summer
drops from her bedroll to the cheap parquet.

Hearing it on holidays or week-ends
few of us worry, even on Sundays,
the night of the incorrigibles.
Old McCray will buzz his wheelchair
out to the balcony, testing "the *caller* air"
(he has his Burns by heart),
and tell eleven storeys of the world
that "Fuckers nowadays can't hold it;
should still be at the teat."
The prudent touch their doors
to feel for heat. Not finding it,
they sniff at the dusty hallways
in part for smoke, in part for scorn.
Most of us bank the false alarms
with our week's-worth of ill-will,
hardly turning from the narcotic blue
of show-and-sell. But mid-week
the tocsin rings inside one's chest,
the long, slow pulse of megasaurs
out of the sleep museum.

Smoke! McCray rolls onto his balcony.
The diva-that-was, hair lavishly unpinned,
poses, white-robed, on hers.
Some, worn by *belle indifference*,
stay sighing in their chairs.
The rest of us jostle politely
into the narrow stairwells.

The half-lit courtyard brims
with faces already discomposed for night.
Gay couples, gray couples, the uncoupled,
the able and assured clubbing together,
all-sorts manqués, a babe-in-arms
astonished into sleep, an elfin face –
unsorted creatures out of Fortune's ark,
foundered on this downtown street.

The sirens slow to groans.
And all at once the civic pomp
of storey-high red and gold
pumpers and ladder-trucks
becomes the the silent films'
comic hyperbole. Trash fire.
We wanted a real one – not the sham
good news of anticlimax.

Late though it is, we linger,
unwilling to leave the sumptuous
to-and-fro of sudden neighbours.
It is hardly intimacy,
yet that lack is briefly eased
by the too-emphatic greetings,
the conversations that unravel,
the fellowship of clichés –
all glimpses of a plenty
that McCray's taunting, "Suckers!"
and the diva's exit shrug
cannot make more elusive.

Sheeted, inert, disposable as cadavers,
post-surgicals are rolled on noiseless stretchers
out of healing pantomimes of murder.
Freight elevators drop them and their porters
into this garage-like underworld
where each glides to a numbered bay.
Behind them, from a palisade of gauges
a ventilator breathes a cautionary hush.

Here no one called will answer to a name.
Even the secret diminutives
of foreplay and racial slur raise no response.
This is particular space, empty of fantasy,
where the numberless laws of molecular domains
are executed without agents in uninvented time.

Routinely, nurses walk the bays,
touching a flaccid cheek or foot;
two interns scan a chart,
exchange a formulaic phrase:
the world as the conscious find it cloys.

One sleeper, then another, stirs.
The room coagulates out of light,
and from the cold retreat of anaesthesia
shadows of pink and white
resolve in consoling shapes:
the ripeness beneath a uniform,
the bonework of a hand,
a leaning tower of plastic cups.

Gradually the morning's cohort wakes,
resuming civic faces.
Time accelerates fitfully from arrest
toward the halfspeed of convalescence.
Somewhere nearby, a cardiac monitor,
still urging caution,
cheeps loudly, like a cardinal in flight.

AUBADE

Gray-fingered light pries at the slats of the jalousie.
Outside it is silver and blue, and drifting white
on the glass chorale of downtown towers.
Hotel flags dangle famous ideas above the traffic
as Japanese tourists step from limousines,
gingerly setting foot on the exotic.
On wake-up radio Haydn seems almost Mozart,
yet less intrusive, the habit of long serenity.
I stretch and yawn, appraised by my daughter's picture
whose cryptic self-possession at age three
is unfolding as solicitude. I find my slippers:
soon the ghostly fragrance of steeping tea
and the solace of butter melting on warm toast.

How rarely the moment is grave or passionate or noble –
for which, with gratitude, I wake again
to an ordinary morning.

TWO

for Agnes and Richard Howe

Unsaturated red, eye-blue, rain-gray –
embroidered arrows, orbs and squares –
the necktie I put on recalls

the Constructivists we admired.
Indulging my stoop-shouldered vanity,
one of you, most likely both together,

bought it at Arfango's a dozen years ago,
a token from our heart-city.
Richard is dead five years now,

Agnes longer, and unfamiliar mourner's eyes
in a familiar face stare from the mirror,
seeing the Gordian knot still taut.

1 : For Denton Fox, medievalist

Gasping at the January wind, I turn away
from the sleet and slobber of University Avenue
into the narrow lobby of Mount Sinai –
its humid warmth close with morning bustle,
ammonia and the cordial odor of coffee.
No need for concern, old friend, this is my yearly:
the numbers benign, the undersea shadows tame –
a friendly thump, and I'm dismissed to live.

Eight years have passed, yet every time I come here
I think of that laggard three o'clock I waited,
resisting thought, outside the diagnostic suite
till Ruth came running, breathless: "Inoperable."
Nothing, no options, not even the maiming salvage
that would have robbed your speech; a few hoarse weeks,
pain – largely druggable – befuddled death.
Time for good-byes and "putting things in order,"
though your things always were.

I'd been your department head, then you were mine.
Unfair exchange: my dozen choice journeymen,
your hundred-odd divas and drudges; my luck,
the 50's tide that floated all careers,
yours, the fiscal ebb. I flattered myself my lot
was Erasmian laughter; yours, an idea of the Good
that darkened to dismay at the gall and greed
seen clearest from the top by "the giver of rings."
Our goddess was Fortuna (street name: Dumb Luck),
blindly dispensing office and disease.

But you were a mountain-climber, with a knack
for dire holds. How self-possessed you were,
already speaking with a raven's caw,
when you ticked off projects that you'd never finish,
and who might take them on – a roll-call
of the gifted and the able from which your absence
was already death. But how to parcel out
the web of thought, the climber's care, the reserve
that sweetened irony, the rueful decency?
Scholars who write on Henryson and Dunbar
go as to a banquet to your work,
and students labour to obey its Gloss:

> *Winnow.*
> *Doubt.*
> *Re-think.*
> *Decide.*
> *Forbear.*

2 : For Peter Marinelli, Renaissance Scholar

Behind you the stylish college grays out of focus.
You are leaning against a low retaining wall,
your rump eased delicately onto the capstone.
You glow with the latest outrage ("can you be*lieve*?"),
and without greetings go headlong into talk,
hands wagging in simultaneous translation.
At the center of the drama is your paunch –
shirted, of course, but benevolent and cheery.

We used to meet by chance at the Wellesley bus stop –
two quidnuncs whose proper office was just such a place:
enough passers-by to prompt our rude speculations,
but too few to muddle fancy with sociology.
Our post, you called it. What heady hours –
you a Sheherazade of gossip, I credulous and enthralled.

It is now some consolation to imagine you
presiding over the Elysium of Scandal
where flapper Did-It-Alls with brass marcels
and rakehell courtiers of Bad King Charles
blush at your stories of conniving deans
and stallion nights among the professoriat.
Or perhaps you reign in Pluto's four-star kitchen,
where Escoffier submits the menus for your approval
and Apicius is taking notes.

At a public time I said the public words
that placed and praised you, but not the man
I met with joy and parted from with laughter,
and shall not meet again, though I perfect
my sorrel soup and learn to tell a tale.

THE ASPARAGUS FEAST

for Dona

1

Fugitive milky blue of a Chesapeake morning,
shimmer of porch screens, chirp of tired wicker.
We dawdled over breakfast planning dinner:
corn from a stand, Red Wonders from the garden,
crab and asparagus gathered from Luck's larder,
your biscuits, of course, with Macs and cheddar later,
and the plonk that Decker and Annette would bring,
pleasant enough after a second glass.

We pitched our crab traps into the tidewater creek,
then, dressed like twins in chinos and white tees,
intimate as a pair of eyes,
we hiked to the old farm. Asparagus
had seeded the edges of abandoned fields.
Not native, yet it had the native's grasp
of soil and weather, flourishing unbidden
in tender, earth-green wands,
promising an underworldly tang.
Another week and all would go to fern
as tremulous as sea-life, firstlings of creation
still resisting the division into elements.

We piled the crabs, steamed orange now and dripping,
on a table covered with *The Sunday Times,*
piled the corn in pyramids and poured the wine.
Dismembering and eating, we said little,
and when our eyes would catch the sorry news
of other worlds, it did not move us –
Decker and French Annette and you and me –
sated on the grace of earth and water,
on touch and touch returned.

2: July Letter

Not the hackneyed autumn
of bounty and recollection,
but July's hypnotic heat
recalls our early, unshadowed
years in that sea-climate
that seemed all breeze and noon;
we two, running handfast,
as much at home as shorebirds,
our need for one another
a fortune earned by spending.

Long since, our rage and grief
have gone as quiet as our flesh,
but love recalls its where and when
as clearly as a snapshot,
yet no more than snapshots tell
of afterward or why. Behind us
there arose a fictive country
of comeliest and best,
where one uses only the *tu*.

3: Lung Cancer

Despite the ads for that perfume
you wore almost to the end
(poor lobes, small graces
spared from the withering),
passion was not everything.
(You had never thought so).
Nor were ambitions, dwindled to privacy;
nor things – you left too many
of the hardly-used, the never-opened,
tokens of unmet occasions.
They were not everything;
at the end a breath was all,
thrashing in its cage.

Near the bouy where the racing dinghies
beat to windward, always your best tack,
we can scatter three kilos of your calcined bone,
say much and weep and drink and not have done with it,
the dark-blonde presence of your mornings
on the balcony in Nice,
at ease with a second coffee,
humorous and favoured in my new robe,
raising your cigarette in that actorly gesture
one knows from playbills,
as wraiths curl upward with your breath
into the clot-red bougainvillea.

4: The Backscratcher

Long as a forearm, yellowed, skeletal,
the grip-end shaped like fisted knuckles,
the working end three claws of split bamboo;
useful, clever, slightly comical –
an intimate allusion everyone gets at once.

Our daughter found it after her mother died,
a small pathos among silk scarves
and the good jewelry in velvet boxes.

I wince at the image of her ungainly comfort,
seeing the innocent places for so long
neither of us could reach.

I closed the curtains, stars shone through;
closed the shutters, heard the gulf's low booming;
locked the windows, still they hummed the wind.

We lay in a seaward room of The Small Marseilles:
stars pinking the gauzy curtain,
the shadowy balustrade a stone ballet,

antic wind at the windows and shutters,
and you, warm length beside me,
your dreaming caught up in a sigh.

Against your waking, I had turned three locks.
Then the thought of last seeing her – that other –
shook me upright like summer thunder.

I had not thought of her in so many years,
all of them ours. So close her gesture
that I rose up shaking, your warmth subsiding on me.

Curtain, window, shutters, I opened the three at once.
Only relenting wind and the rinsing ebb.
It is a summons to spirits, locking up.

Hearing you speak to children,
I learned the language
                    of delight,
its hesitant gestures,
its tenderness in exhortation.

"Regali per tutti!"
        As breathless as the smallest,
        I closed my eyes and held
                            my hand out,
        your offered hand
        the gift I wished for.

"Calma te!"
        We tried, but couldn't
        after we had exchanged
                            our rash confessions,
        regret for regret,
        self-possession for possession.

"Non si tocca!"
        At last we did – touching
        patiently, our hearts
                            in our mouths
        as the little wood near Grève held its breath
        with ours until the hunters passed.

Its organ of eloquence removed,
the vulturine head, tongueless,
bald, crumpled by "further procedures,"
blots out the memory of her face,
estranges the snapshots in the closed album.

A shade even in dreams,
she persists as a wreath of language:
prescient solicitude, endearments,
painters' talk, cooking talk, talk of pleasures taken,
of the bliss and sorrow of ill-chosen attachments.
Speechless, she becomes what she had spoken.

Once she woke me in the streaky dark
to savour one of her delights –
"larks against bells," she called it.
We carried our coffees down to the minty garden
and waited ankle-deep in dew.
Across the shallow valley,
the early traffic crept in glimmers
through the groundmist. At dawn
the cannonade of bells from the Certosa –
as she had promised –
did not drown out small songs.

Birds dumbfounded in their trills by mine,
lions, at a twang, gone mute as hares –

all of it merely critics' self-importance;
soon enough one learns how praises end.

In Hell, Unending Nature sang even louder,
and the damned were in good voice.

When longing for her and my unbelief
whirled me round to face that ravaged shadow,

I alone was silent;
but when I turned away I sang.

Rain is falling, falling tonight on Amsterdam.
Steady, persistent, it does not slant or swirl.
Obeying the hundred laws and a thousand accidents,
it falls without flaw:
luminous beads unstrung from lamplight,
shrugged from the capes of trees.

It sifts a fine gray bloom on roofs and sills;
it drifts over homely districts,
clouding the privacy behind pearled windows.
Canals affirm the acquiescence of water;
cobblestones close wet eyelids against the rain,
now almost an exhalation, a sigh without sound.

If these are tears, they are tears of finer creatures
for sorrows less particular than ours.
The droplets fall, numerous and one,
like words in a story. No clock strikes.
Up to the end it is still a comedy.
But tonight the rain is falling on Amsterdam.

THREE

"THE GUESS OF MEMORY"

LOOKING BACK AT US

for Murray

Today at the Farmers' Market not the expected
Inca musicians piping for small change
but three good Christian men in overalls
playing old-time Country on old gui-tars
and a pawnshop fiddle, raising a jaunty ruckus
that brought back Carolina in a rush:
the worn-down steps of the Durham County courthouse
where the Reverend J.C. Bunn preached Life Eternal
as he handled two of God's own rattlesnakes
till he was cuffed by the World's Most Careful Cops;
and you and Slivia and me and D,
and nights with medico-literary pals
on Med Lab alcohol and dialectic,
arguing that every pain had causes
and Thought could make a summer of the world.

Sometimes, wrote Auden, on leaving a different South,
one knows one has been happy, but not why.
We thought that we knew both.

Across the used-up years I see those days
without envy or condescension, without pride
in meanings later glimpsed or hopes retrieved.
I think of the toad-eyed senator whose guile
once tainted public discourse with the phrase:
"facts, which if proven true." How apt it seems
now for the darkening retrospect
through which we try to summon joyous days.

Fire-scarred and balky, our scruffy troopship
had clambered up and down the swells all morning,
her welded bulkheads belly-aching, even
at going home, when the baritone profundo
of ship's command boomed through the P.A. crackle
with the piety of victories remembered:
"Gentlemen, we are entering the Coral Sea."
That we had crossed a numinous boundary
the Navy knew by arcane instruments.
To the citizen army it was all Pacific
from Tokyo Bay to San Diego: no lines to breach,
no points to hold, a no-man's-no-land
that chug-a-lugged destroyers.
If there were dead here, they had left no cross;
if spirits, they had flown back to the land.
The Coral Sea surrounded us completely,
featureless, indifferent, cold in dreams,
like peace, toward which we sailed.

RECALLING THE ROLL:
HAMPTON INSTITUTE
1955/1995

for Charles H. Nichols

I'd learned them precociously, like sins:
"high yellow," "octaroon," and "spade" –
the white taxonomy for the skins
of chattels Massa flogged or laid.

Now I day-dream down the roll:
tea-rose, cinnamon and coal –

hardly less of an offense
against Boggs, Emory, and Hale,
Holland, Jackson, Pegram, Vance –
names from plantation bills of sale.

Essays blind-graded, surnames placed
on the overleaf – still uneffaced

after four decades that some made
heroic – I see the careful rows
of script, and feel the rage conveyed
by moving, if indifferent, prose.

Studillac, Fuick, Chevrolash, Chrysoto:
Burbank dreamed them just before he died.
Hooded like gryphons, like the mermaid tailed,
sounding the centaur's educated neigh,
they hit the town square, thirty-five in second,
then round and round, moths for brutal neon,
their headlights moons for People's Cut-Rate Drugs,
then round with tires baying at the curbs,
and round again and out.
                              Who hid the girls?

Their birth confounds legitimate Detroit:
carbs with as many chambers as a six-gun,
Hollywood mufflers with a first-night claque,
pennies in the risers, double-jointed pistons,
Barnum gears, a crew-cut engine head.
We said a Requiescat for this junk,
but iron Lazarus, newly sprung from rust,
is carrying his tombstone in his trunk
for getaway.
                              Whereat we elders tut.

The half-breed is always the villain. Sneaks the maps
to Sitting Bull, bootlegs kerosene
(cut with a little whiskey) to the chief.
But fascinating! eyes like deuces wild!
The Colonel's daughter, saved a night too late
and bundled off back East, brings forth quadroons
who people Texarkana, Kiowa, Calexico,
invent the cocktail, the double-take, the old one-two,
colossal corn,
                    and other united states.

THE HUNT

for Harold Fletcher

Call out those gong-mouthed Braques,
French pointers, nobility and barely civil,
but always mad to hunt:
the bitch Caline des Arvernes,
whom well-thighed Vasco got on Tita;
the dog Elan du Therinet,
dropped by Astrale after she had been served
by no less a dignity of flesh
than Xobis de Vamplouisie.
Those two can wrinkle through tall grass like fume,
and mottle into their lagging shadows.
Their sires, both vehement at stud,
willed all their getting a pedantry of scents,
and how to warble from the chest for gobbets.
This is pheasant weather; call them out.

Fletch, loose the dogs, and we with guns on safe
will climb to the right-of-way of the Nickle Plate,
cramped in our last war's clothes and second thoughts
and the will of dogs, habitual as the tracks
but not divided like ours,
who praise our clumsiness for being fair
and slow to learn a prey. The bitch is pointing.
Birds have mated here, begetting heirs
with no more pedigree than a breakfast.
And now the dog, his head an antique bull's,
points, too. The sport is small regrets.

Steady-eyed, silk-tied,
bald, styled, implanted, dyed,
looking like they never lied;
New Dealers, ward-heelers,
county fair- and mall-spielers,
Honest Johns and scene-stealers;
unlikely saints, tailored schmucks
making it on daddy's bucks;
some decent, necessary hacks;
fourteen women, fewer blacks;
Left, Center, Absent, Right –
they hang together in black and white;
panel to ceiling, wall after wall,
they fill the Grill and entry hall
in rows all perfectly aligned,
matted, framed, and boldly signed –
a thousand worthies of the land,
handsome or sinister or bland;
and, still in storage, double those;
dust them, and three thousand pose,
patriots *moyen sensuels*
for whom no minstrel raptures swell.
They did a skeptical country's chores,
brokered her ephemeral laws,
denounced or cheered her doubtful wars
to brief applause,

now turned to indifference or surmise
or mild discomfort at those eyes,
unblinking, overseeing all,
portentous as the Chinese Wall,
guardian presences who watch
over the crabcakes and the Scotch.

A dozen floors above this place
some Highness dines in state, a face –
like Caesar Augustus' or Uncle Joe's –
that even the smallest schoolboy knows
in countries of a single face.

THE AMERICAN SMILE

"The pure products of America go crazy."

– William Carlos Williams

The pure products of America keep smiling, widening
    their mouths, showing gums and molars, and generally
    brightening up.
They smile for the print media, and flash the obligatory
    smile for TV.
You can almost see the smiles coming over on all-news
    radio.
Citizens smile in their daily encounters, as though they
    are posing for billboards.
The clerk smiles at the customer, the customer at the
    clerk,
The teacher smiles and the pupils smile back.
In jostling crowds there are smiles all round.
I see America smiling, the varied smiles, etc.
Is this some infectious mania, Dr Williams,
or have air-borne pollutants combined to form nitrous
    oxide?
The farmer smiles at the cow. Does the cow *know*
    something?
Does everyone smile as much as everyone else, and if not,
    why?
Do sociologists and shrinks, all notable smilers on talk
    shows, have any data?
Is there no avoiding this ubiquity of smiles?

The TV chef smiles as she says that the white truffles of
   Alba are now available only in Alba, so the recipe is
   useless.
The eyewitness smiles when describing the catastrophe,
   and the reporter smiles in encouragement.
The casualties are in bags, so there is no way of telling if
   they smiled on impact.
Is it that we all want to be loved, or to put our best foot
   forward, or don't want to let down the side?
Everyone is having fifteen minutes of fame, fourteen of
   them smiling.
Will there be more late-breaking smiles, or is the message
   out there so bad that nobody wants to risk being shot
   as the messenger?
Or is there really something to smile about, and we go to
   bed wholly remiss with our little grimaces and glooms?
And you, Dr Williams, was it the chronics and
   munchausens and the endless round of truly sick
   people who made you so grumpy,
or only the critics, who smile for professional reasons?

FOUR

He and his friend Hans-Peter, both nineteen, were idling on the Kudamm, following two pleasant pairs of ankles which had stopped at a milliner's window to let the lads catch up gracefully, when an uncle – not much older than himself – appeared at his elbow, and without so much as – Sorry, you're needed at home – hurried him off.

A few steps, and his uncle whispered, "You have one hour to pack." And so, two days before Kristallnacht, the baby of the family left Berlin and was off to America to become the sole survivor. He volunteered for the war and for the infantry, but survived. Afterward he became a civil servant and married a young lawyer who was all one could ask for in a wife, if asking is how one goes about such things. On retirement, he proposed a trip to Berlin, but was only a little displeased when Evelyn decided to remain at home.

In a cafe on the Kudamm, he began a conversation with a woman who was charmed by his old-fashioned German, the idioms of her youth. Soon he had entered an intimacy he hadn't known in marriage. He half-expected Evelyn's bland fairmindedness: no outrage, few demands, and an annoying lack of curiosity. His pension and Magda's income from the hat-shop would do them nicely. And so he resumed his life as a Berliner as though, apart from small linguistic changes, nothing had intervened between the breaking of glass and the melting of cities. Except, except – but he had double-locked all that.

War stories: horrors of combat, horrors of the camps, fantasies and nightmares of luck, dramas of victory and defeat. "Our history is brave, noble and tragic," wrote Apollinaire, but that is the liveried history of governors and tyrants. It is not *our* history, which is ambiguous and banal and the only history we believe. And when we are drawn into *their* history, we curse it for the bloody nuisance that it is, even as we brush our costumes for the walk-on parts.

i

It lay asleep in history, asleep in archives or in the memo-
ries of those who could not sleep; it was known, but
nothing most of us had to live with. Katyn was once a
rumor about a forest; Belsen a certainty, but dismiss-
ably Teutonic-nasty. Then headline by headline, cap-
tion by caption, the photos of human woodpiles
became the family portraits. A crowded ditch stretched
east from Babi Yar to the skull warrens of Cambodia,
north to Manchukuo, south to East Timor, west across
the Gulag to the shallow charnels of Bosnia, south to
Rwanda, north to the ancient bogs where young and
old were garotted, brained and drowned in the modest
numbers of prehistory; then across the Atlantic and
through the Americas to the tribal massacres and the
temple cities and along the routes of violent settlement.
The earth revolved, furrowed incomprehensibly, like
Mars.

ii

Had something gone wrong for him at the Ministry: a
cynical quip, a misstep? He was too canny, too self-
possessed. But one day he was gone. Then we heard he
was in West Africa, dealing in arms with both sides –
and (our Marco!) organizing a third. Marco is not his
real name, nor was any name he used. He cultivated ex-

patriates with sly tales of political scandal. Yet the more affable he was, the more remote he seemed, vividly present, not quite touching. From badly lit archives where I read cinquecento history, he offered occasional relief: a drive to Turin, a drive to Rome.

Before the Autostrada one still took the historic route of the Renaissance – Firenze-Roma – no hill without its story, all of which Marco knew, as he knew where to dine well along the way. The rumors had begun, and I went on our last trip reluctantly, but Marco had errands in Orvieto. I could hardly say no to an afternoon with the Signorelli frescos.

The Fiat jolted heavily, renewing my uneasiness, trained in the instant misgivings of cinquecento intrigue. Was he carrying something for the black market? samples of lethal toys for the latest tribal saviour? My first step inside the cathedral was chilly and dark as a blindfold.

iii

Do you know the Brizio chapel? Michelangelo memorized the cool, dry style of its frescos: the careful anatomy, the stagey grandeur of the crowds, the air of unrelenting seriousness. Angels trumpet Final Judgement from the vaulted heights and the wall is peopled. Skeletons loll among the newly-fleshed. This is the Resurrection of the Body. History has rolled off- stage like a flat; the props of civil and domestic life are hoisted out of sight. We have come a moment too late for the grotesque spectacle – the air thick with limbs torn off by justice, war and accident; flesh and sinew seeking out dry bones; beheadings and maimings flying toward restoration.

Here is humanity reborn perfected, as Aquinas taught: all handsome, all sound of wind and limb, all just 30 – modestly sexed, almost as an afterthought. Some raise their eyes to the commanding clamour, some climb from caskets, some pull others from the earth. The rest stand about stiffly, as alike as mannequins – actors who have forgotten the script of life: gladness, endearment, sorrow, high resolve. What life could these renew? Would these husbands retrieve their scolds, these wives their bullies? Would Guelph and Ghibelline unearth one another? None had the death-camp eyes of Piero's Jesus risen at San Sepulchro. They had been licked clean, not devoured. This was fable. The corporal truths were on another wall: the Damned Entering Hell. Here was humanity impassioned and unredeemed, bound for the front-line and the lynching-tree, the dungeon and the ditch.

iv

In the long shadows of early evening, Marco was shaking hands in a doorway with someone who left quickly. Now too late for dinner at the lake, we walked to a cobbled square where old men were selling roast porchetta off the spit. Thick slices of the savoury meat dripped into hunks of country bread; the taste of rosemary caught in our mouths. We drank rough wine and chatted in the twilight. Marco knew a workmen's bar for coffee and those twisted bits of dough, deep-fried and sugared, called granny's fritters. Still the Tuscan, he was loyal to the pleasures of the poor.

We drove through the dark, the Fiat again her unburdened self, skittish over the uneven road. With my belly served, I thought that Marco's phone calls might be arrangements for his bed-life, and his packages innocuous. In any case, what would the authorities do about me – a foreigner who read old books and chose his companions badly, as foreigners do? And what would they do about Marco, a small-fry with protectors? And what, if anything, would *I* do about Marco? Grow sanctimonious and drop him? Help some politician with a taste for notoriety take a pen-knife to the Hydra's head?

By the time we reached Rome I had decided against returning to Florence by train. Knives there had always been and clubs, always fists and boots, always stones and fire and the needs of life to be scanted or withheld. What was the point of missing a wildfowl dinner at the lake and some fine gossip about the venality of the great, what point in foregoing the sight of Orvieto from the south – brave, improbable civic flower on its stalk of stone?

FIVE

Weary of Q and A:
"Why can't we recall the plot
of *The Way of the World*,
yet staged, the play is lucid?
You may re-phrase the question.
Do you know the date?"
In town for my doctoral orals,
and sleepless with such conundrums,
I put on robe and slippers
and, not to wake my host and hostess,
friends of friends, I tip-toed
down their faux-Tudor stairway
in search of coffee. Six A.M.
was blinding in the kitchen,
my hostess already up.
Neither *The New York Times* she held,
nor the table-top of rippled glass
concealed her nakedness.
"Coffee?" she asked; a goddess
does not speak in sub-texts.
I nodded. She rose and turned.
The epiphany had begun:
arms brighter than her ring,
breasts and belly to the taste of Solomon,
rosy, hale, and supple.

After a proper breakfast
I left for my adventure
armored in the certainty
that those one can formulate,
let alone answer well,
are rarely the important questions.

They spoke about that island,
old friends whom you do not know
(it has been that long),
nor do they know of you
(nobody wants to hear
what is everybody's story).
I told them where we'd found
the fattest Malpeques,
and where the tawny coves
hide from the corniche.
I told them about the snug
that served martinis in goblets.
But I did not tell the best,
for how could they hope
to find that compliant dune,
or that hug of warm Atlantic
beyond the little delta?
We had carried away
those places on our skins.

i

Words at the threshold: the brittle amenities of coming
   and going, the empty rituals of entryways and the
   cramped good-byes in corridors – deploring an early
   departure, pleading a pressing appointment – at just
   such a barren place the undared afterthoughts of our
   coming and going, by then almost dumb with delay,
   were suddenly spoken, the inmost rising unbidden and
   the spell of banality broken, as words were exchanged
   without will – what our coming and going had meant –
   at a threshold finally crossed.

ii

Long-limbed, with "sides longe,"
like Chaucer's Cressid
all lithe articulation
folding your slender lengths,
bending your forearm upward
to shape "with fingres longe and smale"
the crescents of your hair;
or tucking your legs "long streight,"
as if settling to attend,
seriously, like a schoolgirl;
or standing erect with folded arms,
caryatid ennobling a doorway;
or bare arms upraised
in dance or supplication –
O, white wand.

iii

Unlikeliest of hours, 11 A.M.
While others ease their lot
with decaf and prune danish,
we try Spanish plonk and kisses.
Unlikeliest of lovers,
gamy *"Vale,"* freshest *"Ave,"*
exchanging a gift of drink
for a gift of thirst.

iv

Let's preen each other,
pinch each other's mites,
scratch each other's itches
in hard-to-get-at places,
kiss a small damage,
cherish a defect,
lavish fine words on parts
the other cannot see,
then do and do what's done
by other kinds, and then
let's preen each other.

v

Emblem of our arrangements –
half-on, half-off –
your garment greys and glistens

as lamplight glances
along the lustrous lengths
of fabric and left thigh.

Reading this, O lady of particulars,
you will observe – as if to no one –
"Surely it was the right."

vi

I come to you in dreams,
one of Rouault's archaic kings,
great in years, barrel-chested, grave –
about me the black body-halo
of mortality. My left hand
offers you the tulip,
blood's pouch, the ritual flower.
I incline my head to cover yours,
to end my seeing in your hair.
Then you look up, dear face – malign,
staring in triumph from a wall of weapons,
and I another such in arms. I wake
still famished for illusions,
graceless as trousers on a chair.

"We must die because we have known them,"
not only vestals, sibyls and consorts of pharaohs,

but any of them – ox-legged women of the fields,
matrons bent to their diversions, girls in bud –

their ancient ways learned by rote or in the blood,
ways of glancing deeply and touching without pressure,

of simmering a fever with a shrug.
But we also live – how banal to say it –

(for the self-anointed nothing goes without saying),
because we have known them, and we die no matter
    what,

often later because we have known them,
or think we have known them

if only through the communion of need –
this never-jading emptying and filling –

we who are unknown to ourselves,
which is their lot also, who offer smile for smile.

(The title-phrase is drawn from the sayings of Ptah-
hotep, an Egyptian ms. of about 2000 B.C.; it is also the
title of a poem by Rilke.)

That inelegant repetitive manoeuvre
to which you obscenely condemned me
once when your well-bred inhibitions
and bluestocking eloquence gave way,
is hardly the ultimate deprivation.
Do not believe it, madame. As harbinger of Eros
it merits more open favour and allegiance.
Among self-discoveries, largely dismaying,
it is uniquely congenial, a gateless Eden.
It need not woo or buy, write cheques or poems,
defer to headaches or lunar complaints.
It is undaunted by disparities of person,
class, race, age, faith, politics.
It generates neither infatuation nor offspring,
hence none of the consequent nine-tenths
of the world's high romance and private misery.
Its antiquity attracts no historian; its performance no
    critic.
Yet I cannot agree with the celebrated *philosophe*,
who thought that this, requital's "supplement,"
should logically preempt the rest.
The name I would rather drop is Count Negroni,
an amateur of novel drink. Bedeviling his barman
about a new concoction – (the eponymous drink
    survives) –
the Count tasted, sighed, and with polite regret
concluded, "*Molto bene, Pasquale, ma manca qualcosa …
forse Campari.*" Indeed, something such is missing

from that other heady near-perfection –
again, a bitter edge: the headaches, the disparities,
the sorrows, perhaps the lot. At least the risk.

I am thirteen. My sister Kate is tall, slim, a Head Girl, a
gymnast, a debater – at seventeen beyond the reach of
our parents. She divides the world into winners and
losers; sees me fated to be an ink-stained clerk, a low
earner, one of the worthy dull, yet she lovingly imparts
her survival skills: how to flirt and how to dance. "Your
left foot *there.*" Her strong competent fingers give my
hair a condescending tousle. "Those curls are wasted
on a boy. Now hold me closer."

I am fifteen and wander about in acned solitude. I have
memorized the German words for "ineffable longing";
I savour their sweet heaviness on my tongue. My sister
Kate is an unsprouted four, with a punch-line laugh
that will light up three bad marriages. She regards me
with love and awe. After long coaxing, I allow her to
put her muffin feet on my shoes and we dance to the
radio, awkward as circus bears. I hardly listen to her
questions, but answer, "Some day we can do the
shimmy, but not now." I feel a pang of fearful pleasure
that I bring from somewhere not yet in my life,
somewhere worth dancing to.

This is my sixtieth birthday. My daughter has telephoned
and sent a gift. My son has honoured the occasion by
maintaining his principled silence. My Ex has sent her
annual comic greeting card, and I have survived a

drinking lunch with two senior colleagues. Now
I am being taken to dinner by my sister Kate, a
dour and highly successful forty-three. "My little
chrysanthemum," mother had called her; or, when
Kate was out of favour and out of hearing, "my last
mistake." "You know," Kate says (as she had often said
before), "you were more a parent to me than either of
them." "But you were never my child," (my ritual
answer); "you were my dancing partner. Now, how I
wish I had your years." "O, but you have *had* yours;
you know what they are, no surprises." I think: only
the surprise of your answer. Is she ill, or only dismayed
by the futility midway in the journey? But the beloved
face seems without strain or pallor, an unreadable
openness, very Kate.

As you guessed, I have no sister. I am an only son. No one
intended it. My father, who came from a large family,
was very quiet at my birthdays. My mother would
quote the Virgin Mary in the old joke – "I was really
hoping for a girl." About my onlyness my mother said
nothing. My birth had been difficult, her barrenness its
worst and longest-lasting pain.

"Kate," said my mother. "Why would anyone give a child
such a *common* name when they have so many lovely
Saint Catherines?" *They* were our Irish neighbours.
"Kate is a name for a clerk in the Five and Dime," said
my father. "On Saturday nights," he continued, as if to
caution my imaginary sisters, "Kates wear tight skirts
and dance the shimmy. I'll bet she becomes a

Catherine, and spells it with a K and two a's. She'll come into too much of her mother's moolah to stay plain Kate." – Miss Hepburn was not yet a reigning Kate. Even if she *had* been I would have kept my filial silence.

I thought Kate a splendid name: downright and steady, yet with all the flexiblity and nuance of the feminine: Catherine, with a C or a K, Kitty, Kit, Kate, Katie, also with a y, Cathy, Cath, Catriona, Caitlin. The variations in women's names had an opulence far beyond the possibilities of a William, like the greater opulence and metamorphoses of their bodies. Name-shifters they were, name-shifters and shape-shifters, the intent of their bodies not phallically obvious, but budding and drooping with their life's months and seasons.

I am no particular age. I am a disembodied ear, a crinkled leaf unnoticed beside an arrangement of flowers. I overhear the Kates – not as they speak in the common tongue – but when they are free of the presence of my kind. They speak then of the apparent, how pitiless it is, despite enhancements and mitigations; of the labours of food and drink, of the exquisite degrees of connection and estrangement; of what gives solace, what betrays. Of the fear of bringing forth and its Promethean anguish; and then of sleepless exaltations and defeats, and of the banal necessities of maternal life, lifelong even in the telling.

I understand, not know; sympathize, not feel; or know as
   I know the moon – by rumor and report. Myself
   surrounds me like an atmosphere; I breathe refractive
   error. I know as the reader knows the book – at
   imagination's length.

I am thirteen months old, the age when my pediatrician
   said I should have had a sibling, ideally a sister. I am
   lying on a crisp sheet in the maple crib, near the fig-
   tree window. My Auntie Bea, the youngest of my
   mother's sisters, has come to mind me. She leans over
   the bars, takes my hand and sings to my fingers:
       Dance, Thumbkin, dance,
       And dance, ye merrymen, every one,
       For Thumbkin, he can dance alone,
       Thumbkin he can dance alone.
   My mother puts on her brown coat and hat, coos at me
   and leaves. The front door closes. At once Aunt Bea
   hoists me from my crib and starts to dance me around
   the room. She has abandoned her wee nursery voice,
   and is singing to me in a delicious growl:
       Digga-digga-doo, digga-doo-doo,
       Digga-digga-doo, digga-doo.

SIX

These centaurs and these lapiths are one stone, stone and
the shadow of stone, worked with tools fine as pins,
together with that state goblet which has the fallen
bridesmaid's mouth still near it where it burst when a
centaur's hoof skidded for a purchase over the bloody
dishes as she turned sharply to protect her breast after
the uprooting of his tail, which unsprang two tugging
lapiths, their hands full of the twine-y hair, into the
slice-shaped breakage of some wine-jars; above which a
centaur still browses the lapith bride while another
rears to mount her; for which provocation and answer,
answer and provocation are equally given, as instanced
by fractured pastern and crushed thigh amid much
wedding crockery, some whole, on which a Hymen
toys with amorini and so on out to the congé border,
meticulously gouged; and all preserved millenia with
only a few hairline cracks and small abrasions despite
the rise and fall of states and cities, the rough play of
boys, the passage of plough and harrow, the greed of
agents and collectors, the village incidents and the
great wars, the indifference of governments, quake,
fire, breakage of tackle in loading and unloading, the
slack and pry of seasons – when what slight cause has
split a Zeus; a perverse forbearance still insists these
centaurs and these lapiths are one stone.

Whoop of the axe through the air, through the neck.
The ex-head spills its red necklace
of The Three Estates, which break into bloody tears
on the cobblestones of a republic,
The head follows on a string.
The rest, which is really dead,
turns over in spasms of dark syrup.

The size of the torso impresses the common liar,
hence the term "be-headed." Why not "un-torsoed"?
Was the head-tax conceived in a tibia?
The torso dies at once, the head survives a while
with who knows what reflections.

Headsmen say that a reprobate head
stuck out its tongue at the attending priest,
and another head, more pious or just scared,
sang the "Alma Redemptoris." Soon
the speculative Self shrinks to thing-size,
fighting for room with tongue and teeth
and a clump of tubes. Soon it cannot imagine.
Then hardly go out of itself; for a moment
it achieves the perfect concentration
of the "*ding an sich*,"
ending in that stifling loneliness
before the first howl with which we all begin.

In a clinging mist, sour with city cold,
twelve carabinieri with government mouths,
a bandmaster marching downcast with opulent belly,
massed cornetists blaring a chromium psalm,
squads of bayonets, each swaying beneath its point,
the natty maleness of the cadres and conscripts,
the reverence of the beefy gonfaloniers,
a Boy Explorer marching a chubby dance,
benevolent orders jingling beggars' bells,
seminarians, hitching their serpentine lace,
aging lay brothers, stooped, in beach sandals,
shuffling chaplains bent to their breviaries,
the Knights of Malta, staring, imprudent,
the sorrowing bishops carrying guttering tapers,
delay but cannot prevent
the rented truck which bears the arriving death
inside a black enamelled tenement
at whose gilt corners putti howl without relent
while the engine, expertly tuned,
and the driveshaft purr, content.

The flourishes and downstrokes
of a priestly secretary hand
have grayed in photostat
to the reticence of four hundred years,
letters slanting to the right,
as if bending in a drying western air,
a sapless grass of names.

    Hannah Rooley, 2L, dead of a flux,
    leaves Nicholas, 3, and Will, 4 months.
    The widower, Abraham, 22, a tanner, marries
    Meg Dunnock, 18, who bears Avisa and Henry,
    dying of Alice, buried with her.
    Abraham marries Katherine Woodress, widow, 28;
    is spared to father Peter,
    then dies of a tertian fever.
    Katherine marries Lucas Freminge, another tanner
    and widower, 33, with a daughter, Ursula.

    In later documents, Nicholas and Will,
    then 45 and 42, record their gratitude,
    Nicholas especially to Meg, and Will to Katherine,
    "Ever most motherlie in all things,
    with care alwaies for our good order."
    Ursula names her first daughter Kate, her second Meg.
    Avisa thanks God for the health of her father Lucas.

Yet someone must have shouted the hurrahs at hangings
and lashed the butchered quarters to the gates,
burned the witches and heretics, pillaged the Lowlands,
committed the domestic homicides and forcings.

For all our napalm and zyklon-b,
they were no better than us, the parish folk,
but lacking our cures and greeting cards
and our delegation of indifference,
they may have found it harder
to disentangle death from kindness.

No one will ever feel those minute tremors,
that career of particles
disguised as person, place, and thing.
Whatever we walk on is a kind of water.
It is as though the Material, too,
had an Unconscious, the rudiments
hidden everywhere in the open,
coaxed out also by guileless questions
with estranging answers.

Faint arc of scintillations,
so alien to the world as seen,
and yet that world entirely:
Rutherford, his small brass box,
the Cavendish Laboratory,
Cambridge, Europe, and all else.
Cold revelation! Yet it is folly
to wish it more creaturely,
more our own. Given who we are
and were, even before such knowledge
lent us the eyes and then the hands of gods,
it is a providence that the germ of things
is free of purpose and remorse.

Just before you turned the corner, two blue-gray
    elephants passed by, the younger holding the tail of the
    older with her trunk.
As you arrived at the party, the famous pianist, who was
    visiting the host, finished playing the Waldstein sonata.
You just missed Rita in her cartwheel hat.
It is absurd to point out that you also missed the signing
    of the Treaty of Versailles,
absurd but not insignificant, since everyone misses
    almost everything, and increasingly so.
Set your watch ahead, skip breakfast, shorten those good-
    byes –
but all of us are generally elsewhere, indulging in the
    absence of two elephants,
moving gingerly among the likelihoods, with no ocular
    proof that it was Clemenceau who signed the Treaty.

SEVEN

3 A.M.

Don't tempt me with sleep and "*Es muss sein*," Old
   Horror.
Though mornings bring dry crusts and midnights dregs,
I'll have my glut of days. No clever tricks, please –
clutching my arm to feel the hanging flesh,
whispering gibberish to hint my hearing's poor,
wagging beneath my nose a small-print *Genesis*
to prove my eyes part-plastic, and the right
mirrors of a soul you have no use for.
Worse and still worsening, I'm worth the reaping
despite the bronchial wheeze, the raw inch of stoma
and the little graves beneath the eyes.
No need to cheapen the carcass, to jew me down –
as *your* chosen sort of people like to put it.
I know your taste for the Forthright and the True,
but my three-quarters of this century assure me
that your sort hankers even for the least of mine.
So – until the last, Old Chalk-and-Chatter,
sit you snug beside the bed and keep you mum;
I'll know you're there.

SEPTEMBER LETTER

for Catherine

We were so young it seems a story:
I just discharged, rankless, sleepless,
secure in the slangy certainties.
He was a few years older,
at least his war was worse and longer.
We met at your old place, that rampart highrise
that overhung the river – a vista to gorge ambition:
skyscrapers and projects heroic in the smoke,
unending traffic hung from bridges;
recycled since through slum and upscale suites.

His moustache – RAF, a souvenir leg.
He was something in film. The wife was odd –
money, but always edgy; an urgent whisperer,
hair Shaker plain, child-like and round with child.
Like everyone else, after the baby they moved.
I rarely got inside his perfect manners.

Was it a grown daughter or a later wife
I saw him with on the superhighway,
at one of those fluorescent stops
that sheds a shadowless anonymity
on the food, the time, and the patrons?
But it *was* him, hoisting himself from a green Miata.
I think he saw me, think he remembered something,
but neither of us called or gestured.
Travellers' preoccupations? old men's eyes?
the inwardness one needed, living this half-century?
Of course, of course, but also the death-work
that snips at holding points
until the web collapses through its center.

I regret that I have only your old address.

i

Not many left to call out given names,
the pet-names of childhood,

the nick-names in the platoon,
or to whisper night's diminutives.

Almost no one to repeat
the anecdotes and instances;

attest to graces now outlived;
or say if passions

were requited, or merely brief;
the work an achievement

or just the manner of the day.
Friends and lovers and the rest

are culled out from the present,
leaving behind a second infancy

of shades and solipsism,
that famous blank from which one might

begin again, but for the now
almost unimpeachable witness.

ii

"Things fall apart" (they do) –
go snap like a Commandment,

unravel slowly like the fundamentals,
or wear out like hips or planets.

Loosened from plans and preconceptions,
they regain the particularity of childhood.

All this is discovered in Morandi's etchings –
the familiar once again the strange:

empty jars and bottles in common use,
each solitary in its cross-hatch,

barely gathered into design –
vessels for shadow topped up with a little light.

iii
for Julia

What luck we had; against all odds we met,
you, birth-weary, exquisite, and loud,

not knowing what you wanted, just how to get it;
I, less prepared, learning another ignorance

each time you howled, awake, or stirred in sleep.
Then trial and error till they blurred together

like what we said and what we forbore to say.
Sometimes we allow the two we were

to join us again as guests, quite shy at first,
but greatly indulged and comically chatty.

iv

Past an august old tree I stroll along,
both of us creaking comfortably at the joints,

swinging our arms a bit.
Though disfigured by a wrenching climate

and municipal attention,
the tree looks as though another swig

of this unseasonably balmy light
would green it to the top.

They say that all the seaports of the world
will founder when the poles dissolve

some day in this toxic warmth
that comforts two arthritics.

V

Slowly and with regret bright chances
are dusted off and put away,
props of an amateur theatrical
after the first and only night.
You will not learn Greek –
not Homer's or the Hellas Grill's –
end poverty, or even find your keys.
Ancestral voices prophesy the obvious,
which does not come – only the newly strange:
moments racing free of other moments,
trailing no desire, foreshadowing no task.

vi

The chortle of the boy-baby
tossed up and caught,

tossed up and caught
beneath the fig-tree;

the thump of volleyball
after gunfire;

the intimacies breathed
and the banalities of separation

all hold in a long sostenuto,
clearer than first heard.

Extravagant meanders
loop through the long-eroded plain,

glittering into dusk,
while newer sorrows and delights,

some equally painful now,
wink out like fireflies.

vii

The hour is over. I gather my books to leave
as I did after classes in those bright, small rooms –

where again such brightness, such closeness? –
almost at peace with a few of the works discussed,

with guilty doubts, as ever, about the others –
did I misread? impose? was I too clever? –

I wait for the questions that always occur
to everyone later on – but leave at last,

after suggesting this topic, which may seem,
though not for long, irrelevant to the texts.

Hair and skin one whiteness, eyelids locked,
his stillness is the stillness of the bedclothes;
his words, not speech but systems emptying out:
Death is taking back the small distinctions
between man and man and man and anything.
Gone the treasury of signs and cures,
the warrior ambition to better or sustain.
Now only the heave of managed breath, the lisp
of oxygen, and the dry tears of vigil.
Death, why do you trivialize your only lesson
with idiot repetition? Could you not give
even so gallant an enemy his due:
the coup de grace of massive stroke,
the grudging favour of fatal accident?

OLD MAN AND SKELETON IN
A TEACHING HOSPITAL

(with a first line from Winfield Townley Scott)

How will I ever come to any good
unless I get sorted out and make myself useful?
This fellow here, at last too brief for wit,
proves it possible, even now.
That tower of vertebrae,
more cunningly poised than Pisa's,
shows more balance and coherence
than there is, so far, in me.

Like the rest of the laity,
I pause before instruction.

I can fancy myself as such a consummation,
essential at last, without my innards,
which were a burden (though recently less)
to me and the Chief of Surgery;
and also without my outards,
which were never my best feature.
As for the metaphysical parts,
I see no sign of loss in him
of those inventions of inference.

Upstairs here in PSYCH
it is thought good doctrine
that insight leads to change.
– What insight led to *this*?
Better to think that change can lead to insight,
and learn from this bone-brother
a modest indifference.

EIGHT

NOTES ON SPEECH AND SILENCE

"Speak that I may know thee."

— *Jonson*

If you were here again and nothing more
between us but a cafe table and two *blancs* –
you in that pale blue dress,
Perdita incognita among the idlers –
I'd pour out all I've hoarded; you would, too:
questions, second-and-after-thoughts, and guesses.
Nothing would be unlistened to, unspoken.

I want to hear your ideas on Bruegel's *Icarus.*
We never finished with that 17th-century cleric
who thought of God as a kind of Jackson Pollock
dribbling stars. Or with porism. Or with Tillich.
Words about words, feelings about and in them,
modest but shaping all, like punctuation.

Under the floorboards of a ruined shed
I found a pack-rat's treasure:
scraps of cancelled cheques, a girl's barrette,
the cap off a fifth of Schenley's – neural clutter.
Is my hoarding for unsilence only *this*?
Genetic tic? Mind's self-serving pirouette?
Boundary keepsakes? Debris as reassurance?
Or the disguise of some atrocious need?

When we spoke last you wept, only two tears:
sheen suddenly on the sclera, gathering,
filling the lower rims and brimming over;
drops on the cheekbones flattening to a stop.
The half-dozen words I spoke, loosed from some hell
in me, now stick in my craw, and neither speech
nor silence can unsay them.

To feed off the marrow of straw,
the fat of shale,
the crackling of the beetle's case,
to drink the damp of shade –
how can I trust this organ of fantasy
that thinks of one thing
only to think of another,
that will not part
the seer from the seen,
or either from the seeing –
this muchness that drowns out
the cry of simple want,
even in speaking of famine?

PASTIMES

for John

Like puzzle-pieces springing out of blanks,
peasants forsake the half-tilled fields
and goodwives clap the flour from their hands.
Even the lord of the manor makes himself common
for a sight of these two at their mystery –
Tamblin the Tumbler and Janikin the Juggler.
They are the only gossip –
their dress, their diet, their opinions.
Do they take lovers, or abstain for the sake of art?
Everyone's muscles tremble like sympathetic strings
as Tamblin leaps. The thoughtful sort
think Janikin's far-fetch of club and ball
is more profound, the mind's resilience.
The village priest has prayed for wisdom:
is this God's grace or the Evil One's distraction?
But he sighs when they leave the village.

We fear the drought, we fear the flood,
and plague and witchcraft;
we fear our masters' wars – but not just now,
while Tamblin leaps.

Evocations of the bitter dust of cities,
seaside mornings and the odor of verbena –
pages we skimmed in the famous stories,
impatient with the clutter of place and gesture,
wanting to get on with life and death.
Now we read less, but read more slowly,
having learned to our cost that only in stories
are endings resolutions, resolutions meanings;
that meanings, such as they are,
lie in the pages skimmed –
the crocus spoiling in the vase,
the blind old dog who rose to greet his master,
returned after many years, disguised.

FOR P.K. PAGE

I would not wish for you,
O laureate of precisions,
nor do I think you would accept it,
a large remembrance oxidizing
alongside Former Names,
or a plaque and serious photos
in some underfunded library.
Too loud or too dreary, those.
Instead, a renewable elegance –
like one of your phrases –
but cold as from this country,
and with the tang of exotic travel –
a dark sauce napping an ice of fruit;
so Melba is remembered and Pavlova
in the flourishes of a lesser art,
appeasing a simpler hunger.

(after her poem on Pushkin)

To be known at once and only by a surname
throughout that tongue-tied land
where not to know was safety;
to be known by the initial of her given name,
lower case, decisively lined through
(was she mocking her famous censors
whose names now baffle pedants?) –
to be known as though there had been
no Anna saints or queens, no Annas with a story;
to have the unspoken thanks of those who knew
only by rumor a single affirming phrase she wrote.

At what cost to the favourite
of the Stray Dog Cabaret in her silken sheath,
the dolorosa of "three hundred hours"
before the prison-gates of Moscow,
the sibyl in the exile of silence?
Hunger, typhus, bereavement, siege, and whatever else
the Central Committee and its creatures
exquisitely devised – every cost.

Like Pushkin, she followed to the last
the wayward path of Russian words,
she, toward the bold and the ambiguous –
"thunder" and "shadow," her favourites –
words more substantial now than what they stand for.

(Professor Kathryn Feuer brought the text of Akhmatova's
poem-cycle on the Yezhov terror, *Requiem*, out of the Soviet Union
in 1964.)

Anyone who cared to, knew the story:
this Terror and then that, the criminal legalism,
lives shrugged away and lied into oblivion –
knew it to hopelessness; why take the risk
to smuggle stale bad news?
Or was it less to torture than to poetry
you hoped to bear true witness –
to language, unstilled, untamed,
the inmost voice insisting on itself?

Through Moscow streets you went
with your flimsy treasure of lamentation
into the history of Russian letters,
hoping from us as little notice
as from the KGB. Stalin is gone
and Yezhov and Zdanov and the rest,
but the *apparat* lies dozing on its paws,
awaiting a master's whistle.
If you knew a trick they didn't,
you did well to keep your counsel,
as now, alas, you must.

Standing beneath her hanging cities,
warrens of brush strokes,

tilting forts of saturated colour,
I used to imagine the painter clinically smocked,

gaunt, vatic, Northern, a pillar between gray windows
that repeated in silence a heaving Baltic.

Blonde and brushed, a Head Girl prettiness
tightened to self-possession,

the painter appeared on screen
at no one else's centre;

citizen-bourgeoise, unexceptionally dressed,
only a quiet singleness,

an immunity from occasions, also this one,
hinting at the tumult of raw paint.

These streets have been cleared of our kind. Only a few
rush through their shadows as if to meet a curfew

or, caught in doorways, lean and stare,
awaiting – there will never be one – an all-clear.

Here day is as private as dark, a creatureless sky –
the stagey quiet of a backlot Pompeii.

Granted we're out for ourselves, but this estrangement,
this isn't what we meant.

Perhaps the painter, despite himself, intends
a hunger for opposites in these intense

unmeetings: a longing for streets walked arm-in-arm,
for skies of grackles singing in a swarm.

Unlike the prime de Wints and Callows,
they lean against the walls like loiterers,
unnoticed, merely glimpsed.
But seen when one takes time to see,
they evoke familiar acres, local as a face,
and rutted cart-tracks under a clement moon.
Uncatalogued, unframed, they can tease the looking:
binsful, unsigned, now dusty bargains.

We cannot guess how much or what
this unforgiving art once cost its makers:
unpresentable cousins with habits below the station
to which these were illusory rungs;
exhausted factors who took up the brush
with sea-baths and a brown tonic upon advice;
clerics' daughters cultivating "parts" in lieu of dowry;
misses on the verge of appropriate lives
for whom these were their longest free consideration –
painters devising elsewheres.
In the bulbous clutter of the age
there was spaciousness in imagined fields,
candor in imagined faces.

Picky work, these knacks of dilute umber
translated to hill or bridge,
yet finally serious, exacting hard decisions.
Cruder strategies and less passion
put down the Luddites or the Sepoys,
unearthed the secret beginnings of the Nile,
achieved the Port-fame of the willing and well-hung.
But these, also inscribed on water, outstay their medium,
affixed to paper that browns and withers
more slowly than the treaty with the Shogun.

They do not jostle, chatter, or block one's view
but, without turning, move aside as though a stir
too subtle for hearing prompted their politeness.
The intimacies of shadow and the passions
of colour seem to catch their eyes at once,
which follow the quiet diamonds of a trellis
up to the combs of thatch. Their hands upraised,
they seem to bless the canvas, signing space
with gestures like the brushstrokes of a painting,
another eloquence denied all sound.

Before we invented speech there was no such silence.
Water purred, hissed, or roared, as did the air;

as fire did when it tired of preening itself.
Even the shadow of a passing cloud

trailed updrafts that whirred through grass.
But the spoken life is clogged with silences:

the unsaid, the forborne, the implied,
the passionately – or merely – inarticulate.

A child falls silent, sensing he's not best loved,
not even sometimes favored. A young painter stands

mute before the canvas, facing all at once
the burden of her gift. A deserted wife

purses the blood from her lips and will not cry out.
Our self-recognitions too are often unspeakable.

Some courting language, some with no known
    translation,
the silences huddle together like thirsty shades

in classical hells, bloodless and transparent –
or like sheets of paper, waiting, blank.

RESPECTS TO WILLIAM BASSE
(1583?-1653?)

"Renowned Spenser, lie a thought more nigh
To learned Chaucer, and rare Beaumont lie
A little nearer Spenser, to make room
For Shakespeare ... "

i

Vertebrae clicking like a Geiger counter,
gloom and charnel odors as the distinguished
remains scrape sideways. Are the skulls a-gape
with scorn or welcome? Do the elbows chip?
Bizarre and banal, yet Basse had it right.
New poets enter, everybody shifts,
even for Basse – move over, elegists.

ii

Pope's sequiturs are re-routed
for the Ashbery parade.
Though Chaucer's Prioress
declines to step aside for Milton's heaven,
the news is not all bad: Tsvetaeva
and De Musset match shades of disappointment
to their mutual advantage.
Wordsworth improves Traherne.

iii

Even the best hold still for the raven's beak.
Would Basse or even Chaucer himself
recognize the music of his "*Prologue*"
in the best-guess brogue philologists recite?
Allusions turn to labours then to riddles;
times change and a nuance withers to a gloss.
Reader, only the poets of your day
make poems of your thought and speech;
read them; only you can read them truly.

ACKNOWLEDGMENTS

Versions of several of these poems have appeared in *Accent* and *The Dalhousie Review*, "The Hot-Rods Ride at Dusk" was published in *The Nation* (1957); "Insomnia" appeared in a different form in *Poetry* as "Light Bulb: Lares"; iv from "Toward Winter" ("to Julia") was published as a 1998 Gauntlet Press broadside by Barbara Howard and Richard Outram.

I am indebted to many friends, but chiefly to Al Moritz, John Reibetanz, and M.L. Rosenthal; to John Allen, Nancy Lindheim, Brian Parker, Hugh Anson-Cartwright, Annette Tromly, and Lally Grauer; and to Tracy Ware, my editor; and to Nathalie Cooke, Stephen Dinsmore, Susanne McAdam, and Joan McGilvray of the Press. Susan Glickman and Jay Macpherson bravely read an almost final draft.